RED-TAILED HAWKS

DOUG WECHSLER

The Rosen Publishing Group's
PowerKids Press™
New York

To Rog, may the red-tailed hawks always munch on the voles in your fields.

About the Author
Wildlife biologist, ornithologist, and photographer Doug Wechsler has studied birds, snakes, frogs, and other wildlife around the world. Doug Wechsler works at The Academy of Natural Sciences of Philadelphia, a natural history museum. As part of his job, he travels to rain forests and remote parts of the world to take pictures of birds. He has taken part in expeditions to Ecuador, the Philippines, Borneo, Cuba, Cameroon, and many other countries.

Published in 2001 by The Rosen Publishing Group, Inc.
29 East 21st Street, New York, NY 10010

First Edition

Book Design: Michael de Guzman

Photo Credits: p. 4 © A. Walther/VIREO; p. 7 © F. Lanting/VIREO; p. 8 © B. K. Wheeler/VIREO; p. 11 © John Cancalosi/VIREO; p. 12 © B. K. Wheeler/VIREO; p.15 © T. Vezo/VIREO; pp.16, 20 © B. K. Wheeler/VIREO; p.19 © F. K. Schleicher/VIREO; p. 22 © S. J. Lang/VIREO. All photographs from VIREO (Visual Resources for Ornithology), The Academy of Natural Sciences' worldwide collection of bird photographs.

Wechsler, Doug.
    Red-tailed hawks / by Doug Wechsler.
        p. cm.— (The really wild life of birds of prey)
    Summary: Introduces red-tailed hawks and describes their physical characteristics, habits, and life cycle.
    ISBN 0-8239-5596-6 (lib. bdg. : alk. paper)
    1. Red-tailed hawk—Juvenile literature. [1. Red-tailed hawk. 2. Hawks.] I. Title.
  QL696.F32 W425 2000
  598.9'44—dc21   99-059154

Manufactured in the United States of America

CONTENTS

DOUG SAYS

FEW BIRDS CAN LIVE IN AS MANY DIFFERENT PLACES AS THE RED-TAILED HAWK CAN.

THE EVERYWHERE HAWK

Red-tailed hawks live nearly everywhere across North America. They fly over farm fields. They soar over cities. They glide over the mountain ridges. About the only place you cannot find red-tailed hawks is on the cold **arctic tundra** of Alaska and northern Canada. In North America, they like almost everything but dense forest. South of the United States, they live in the mountains as far away as Panama in Central America.

Red-tailed hawks are large hawks. They are about 4 feet (1.2 m) across from wing tip to wing tip. This length is their **wingspan**. Stretch your arms out and compare that to your "wingspan."

The adult red-tailed hawk has an unusual reddish brown tail. Young red-tailed hawks have brown tails with narrow black stripes.

WHAT IS FOR DINNER?

Red-tailed hawks are **raptors**, or birds of **prey**. Why are red-tailed hawks among the most common hawks in North America? They do so well because they can **adapt**, or adjust, to their surroundings. If mice are common, the red-tailed hawks will eat mice. If the red-tailed hawks live in the city, they will eat squirrels, pigeons, and even rats. In the desert, they hunt for young rabbits and snakes. Red-tailed hawks are not fussy. They will even eat rattlesnakes. Other popular items on their menu include gophers, ground squirrels, ducks, and **carrion**. On Socorro Island, off the coast of Mexico, their favorite food is land crab.

Red-tailed hawks are not picky about what they eat. They will eat mice, pigeons, squirrels, and even rattlesnakes.

DOUG SAYS

RED-TAILED HAWKS FEED MOSTLY ON MAMMALS.

HIGHWAY HAWKS

Did you ever notice a large hawk sitting near the highway? Chances are it was a red-tailed hawk. Roadsides are good places for a red-tailed hawk to hunt. Most roadsides do not have trees, so the hawk can see mice and rabbits move through the grass. Telephone poles, light poles, and signs all make great **perches**. From there, the red-tailed hawk can spy its prey. Next time you drive through the countryside, look for these hunting hawks.

Red-tailed hawks use telephone poles and other high perches so they can easily spot prey.

High in the arms of a giant cactus, a pair of red-tailed hawks builds a nest of sticks. After laying three eggs, the pair **incubates** the eggs for four to five weeks. The female usually keeps the eggs warm, but the male pitches in, too. He does most of the hunting and brings back food for the female.

It takes several hours after hatching for the young to raise their heads. By the second day, they start to move and to peep. The male brings food to the nest in his **talons** about 15 times per day. The female's job is to **brood** and feed the young. She broods by covering them with her body and wings. This keeps them warm or shades them from the hot sun.

For the first four weeks, the female tears off little bits of meat from the prey and offers them to her hungry young.

DOUG SAYS

WILD RED-TAILED
HAWKS HAVE
BEEN KNOWN TO
LIVE TO BE 21
YEARS OLD.

LEARNING TO BE A HAWK

About the same time the young start to eat on their own, they begin flight training. They stretch their wings and flap. They practice for two weeks in the nest before taking the big leap. Once out of the nest, they stay nearby for the next three weeks. Soon they begin to soar on their own. They have only a few short weeks to learn to hunt before their parents stop bringing them food.

◀ *A young red-tailed hawk that has learned to fly soars in the wind.*

SIT AND WAIT

The red-tailed hawk is a sit-and-wait **predator**. That means it perches someplace with a good view and waits until it sees a small animal. When it does, it spreads its wings and swoops toward its prey. With powerful talons it grabs its victim. Then it bites the neck to kill it. If the prey is not too big, the red-tailed hawk will fly to a perch with dinner in its talons. The red-tailed hawk prefers to dine in the safety of a tree or pole.

At times, the hawks take to the air to hunt. They fly over fields in search of food. If they see a mouse or other prey, they dive quickly and grab it before it can escape.

A red-tailed hawk likes to eat its prey on a perch where the hawk is safe. If the prey is a large animal, it will eat it on the ground.

STAY OFF MY LAND!

During the breeding season, a pair of red-tailed hawks does not like company. The pair protects its land from other red-tailed hawks. The land the pair defends is called a **territory**. A red-tailed hawk will chase or even attack another red-tailed hawk that flies into its territory. The pair knows the territory well. The pair usually stays together until death, and may keep the same territory for many years. By defending a territory, the pair keeps other hawks from eating the animals it will feed to its young.

A red-tailed hawk carefully guards its territory. It will even chase away another red-tailed hawk that flies into it.

MIGRATION

In the colder parts of the United States and Canada, from northern British Columbia to New England, food becomes scarce in winter. Some prey, like meadow mice, tunnel beneath the snow where hawks cannot catch them. Others, like chipmunks, **hibernate** deep in holes in the ground.

The hawks must move on to better hunting grounds. In late fall, hawks that live in the cold north **migrate** to the south where it is warmer. They fly along mountains and over lakes. In November and December they reach their winter homes in the southern United States. They share these areas with the southern red-tailed hawks that do not migrate.

When a red-tailed hawk migrates, it flies along mountains and over lakes. ▶

DOUG SAYS

SOME RED-TAILED
HAWKS MIGRATE
AS FAR AS 2,000
MILES (3,226 KM).

HAWK HABITAT

Every animal has a **habitat**, or a place that provides it with the right type of food, shelter, water, and space to raise its young. A red-tailed hawk is the kind of animal that is called a **generalist**. A generalist can have many different habitats. It is not fussy about where it lives. Its habitat can be the desert, the prairie, the woods, or even the city park. It does have some special needs, though. The red-tailed hawk must have a high place to nest, like a tree, a windmill, or a rocky cliff. It needs an open place to hunt, like a forest clearing, city dump, or grassland. It also needs a tall perch where it can watch for prey.

A red-tailed hawk is happy to spy from a fence post, a dead tree, or a huge rock. It needs a high perch to watch for prey.

WATCHING RED-TAILED HAWKS

You do not have to stay on the highway to watch red-tailed hawks. Most large city parks have red-tailed hawks, at least in winter. You could also try to find one at an old cornfield in the fall. The cornfield will probably have lots of mice. You can bet a hawk will want to visit a field full of mice!

The best time to see a lot of red-tailed hawks is during fall migration. In the eastern United States, migration peaks in October and November. In the western United States, keep your eyes on the sky from September to October. It can be really exciting to see one red-tailed hawk after another fly by. It is also nice to know that with so many bird **species** in trouble, this is a bird that is doing well.

GLOSSARY

adapt (uh-DAPT) To change to fit new conditions.

arctic tundra (AR-tik TUN-druh) Land with grasses, low-growing plants, and no trees near the northern edge of North America, Europe, and Asia.

brood (BROOD) When a bird covers its eggs or chicks with its body to keep them warm or shelter them from the sun or rain.

carrion (KAR-ee-un) Dead, rotting flesh of animals.

generalist (JEN-er-uhl-ist) An animal that eats many kinds of food, or lives in many kinds of places.

habitat (HA-bih-tat) The surroundings where an animal or plant naturally lives.

hibernate (HY-bur-nayt) To sleep through the winter.

incubates (IN-kyoo-bayts) Keeps eggs warm, usually at body temperature.

migrate (MY-grayt) To regularly move to a faraway place to spend the season.

perches (PERCH-ez) Tree branches or other things on which birds can rest.

predator (PREH-duh-ter) An animal that kills other animals for food.

prey (PRAY) Animals that are food for other animals.

raptors (RAP-terz) Sharp-clawed birds that hunt other animals.

species (SPEE-sheez) A single kind of plant or animal. For example, all people are one species.

talons (TAL-unz) Sharp, curved claws on a bird of prey.

territory (TEHR-uh-tohr-ee) Land or space protected by an animal for its use.

wingspan (WING-span) The distance from wing tip to wing tip when a bird's wings are stretched out.

INDEX

WEB SITES

To learn more about red-tailed hawks, check out these Web sites:

http://www.raptor.cvm.umn.edu/
http://www.id.blm.gov/pobnca/index.html
http://www.acnatsci.org/vireo (Readers can order a raptor slide set.)